Deborah, ARISE!

A SANCTUM + SEED BIBLE STUDY JOURNAL

TuRhonda Freeman

Absolute Author
Publishing House

Sanctum and Seed, a subsidiary of The Free Man Beyond Me Foundation, a 501c3 organization
Website: http://www.SanctumAndSeed.com

Cover design by Jose Pepito Jr.
Back author photo by Ashley Strickland

ISBN: 978-1-64953-054-7

Welcome

Oh, hello there! I'm so glad that you're here. I can't think of any better place for us to be in this moment. Your presence here indicates that you are ready to dig deep into God's Word and hear Him speak in refreshing ways.

You are holding a powerful tool in your hands – one that has been composed to draw you deeper to the well of God's Word. This Bible Study journal is intended to prompt you to peel back the layers of scripture so that you can see how your ordinary life aligns with God's extraordinary plan. Oh, and does He have a plan for you – one that is above and beyond your wildest dreams and expectations.

Because of the depths and richness of God's Word, you'll never run short of treasures to uncover. The S-E-E-D Bible Study method is designed to help you dig. Whether you have 20 minutes or 2 hours, this tool will help to simplify your study time. At the end of the daily reading, there is a S-E-E-D verse to provide a more thorough study. You are welcome to dig as much or as little as you desire. The purpose of those verses is to create a habit of daily-digging. Even if you've read a particular verse a hundred times before, there is always something new to discover.

My prayer for you is this: that you will wear this journal out; that you will work it from every angle; that you will show up, fully present and ready to hear God speak every single time. My prayer is that you will lose yourself in the treasure-hunt of scripture. And that a new woman will emerge – a woman who is well able to rise above any obstacles in her path.

TuRhonda Freeman

Deborah, ARISE!
A BIBLE STUDY JOURNAL

The Lord is commissioning women of this generation to come out of the shadows. No more playing it safe. No more excuses and no second-guessing. You are God's best kept secret - hidden in plain sight. Your days of obscurity, settling for safe, playing second fiddle are coming to an end.

Deborah, Arise! is a spiritual awakening for the modern woman of faith. This study through the life of Deborah will give a fresh perspective to the word "anointing". You will be ignited to Arise!, arm yourself with the grace and grit of God's word, and fulfill the assignment(s) that He has given you. The treasures that are tucked on the inside of you will be uncovered and pushed to the surface. You will learn how God can take an ordinary woman and make her a history-maker and a chain-breaker who will blaze the trail for generations to come. Like Deborah, you'll discover the power of worship and the art of breakthrough. And your potential…let's just say that it'll no longer be hidden.

"Village life ceased, it ceased in Israel, until I, Deborah, arose, arose a mother in Israel." ~ Judges 5:7

Contents

The S-E-E-D
Bible Study Method

$\mathcal{S}$ — (Scripture)

Select one scripture or passage of scripture to focus on. Read it at least 2-3 times.
Then, write it down in a notebook/journal word-for-word.
Then read it once again (preferably out loud), taking your time to allow each word to soak into your thoughts.

E — (Examine)

Dig deeper into the scripture. Pay attention to the context (*history, background, and the larger idea or message*) of the scripture.
Read the scripture in another translation. Read the notes from a study bible or a bible commentary. These tools will help to provide background information and theological explanations that will bring biblical truths into sharper focus.

Find 1-2 cross reference scriptures that support the scripture. The Topical Bible in www.OpenBible.info is a good resource for finding cross reference scriptures.

Lookup the definition of 1-2 words from the verse. Make a note that definitions in secular and biblical dictionaries may differ.

Use a reliable source such as www.BlueLetterBible.org to examine the scriptures in greater depth.

Write down any facts that you've learned from your digging to help you gain deeper insight (perhaps using the Five W's — Who, What, When, Where and Why).

E — (Envision)

What do you see in this verse? How does it speak to you? What are your takeaways from this scripture?

Think about ways to apply this scripture to your life or situation.

D — (Declare)

Turn your thoughts to prayer. Write out a prayer of declaration. Thank God for planting this scripture in your heart.

Here is an example of how to use S-E-E-D in this Bible Study Journal:

(S — Scripture)

Isaiah 12:3 ~
Therefore
with joy
you will draw water
from the wells of salvation.

(E — Examine)

Isaiah's readers doubtless thought of how God satisfied the physical thirst of their ancestors in the Wilderness of Sin (Exodus 17:1-7). The same provision will apply for their descendants when the Messiah comes to deliver the nation (Isaiah 41:17-18; 30:25; 35:6-7; 43:19; Psalm 107:35) The New Testament amplifies this provision to include the supply of spiritual water for the thirsty soul (John 4:10, 14; 7:37; Revelation 7:16-17; 21:6, 22:17)[1]

---

[1] MacArthur, John F. *MacArthur Study Bible*, Thomas Nelson, 1997.

Therefore = means 'for that reason or cause'; What reason or cause? This is where you should go back to the previous verse(s) to trace the thought and establish the context of the scripture. **Isaiah 43:1-2** says - *And in that day you will say:*

"O Lord, I will praise You;
Though You were angry with me,
Your anger is turned away, and You comfort me.
² Behold, God is my salvation,
I will trust and not be afraid;
'For Yah, the Lord, is my strength and song;
He also has become my salvation.'"

According to John McArthur's Study Bible commentary, Isaiah 12:1-3 are 1 of 2 brief songs of praise which redeemed-Israel will sing at the outset of millennial kingdom. They are the earthly counterpart to the heavenly doxology in Revelation 19:6-7 - *And I heard, as it were, the voice of a great multitude, as the sound of many waters and as the sound of mighty thunderings, saying, "Alleluia! For the Lord God Omnipotent reigns! ⁷ Let us be glad and rejoice and give Him glory, for the marriage of the Lamb has come, and His wife has made herself ready."*

Now, you can ascertain that 'therefore' is referring to the promise that God will deliver His bride – the Church and the faithful Israel.

Therefore = because of the promise of a future and final deliverance

with joy =

Before we define this phrase in the English language, let's see how the word was used in the original text. The Interlinear Bible on BlueLetterBible.org is a great resource. An interlinear Bible is a tool that helps identify Greek and Hebrew words with their English translation.

In the interlinear section, you'll find that the original word used for 'with joy' was a Hebrew word: *'sasown'*. Strong's definition for 'sasown' is cheerfulness; specifically, welcome: gladness, joy, mirth, rejoicing.

In the Gesenius' Hebrew-Chaldee Lexicon (*which is a wordbook that takes root words and converts the vocabulary of the ancient text to vocabulary that is suitable with today's language*), you'll find that 'joy' is referring to the oil of gladness, used of the ointments which they used at banquets. The Lexicon points us to **Isaiah 61:3** – *To console those who mourn in Zion,*
To give them beauty for ashes,
The oil of joy for mourning,
The garment of praise for the spirit of heaviness;
That they may be called trees of righteousness,
The planting of the Lord, that He may be glorified."

From Isaiah 61:3, the John McArthur Study Bible points to **Psalm 30:11** ~ *You have turned for me my mourning into dancing;*
You have put off my sackcloth and clothed me with gladness,

Now, we can better define 'with joy' based on the original language and the supporting scriptures.

> **With joy** = with gladness and rejoicing that has replaced
> all mourning and sorrow

you will draw water =

The drawing of water in biblical times was a daily task for women. The first time that 'drawing water' is mentioned in the bible is in **Genesis 24:11** – "And he made his camels kneel down outside the city by a well of water at evening time, the time when women go out to draw water." Drawing water is a feminine and physical expression in the scriptures. A woman cannot expect someone else to draw the necessary water for her household. She must put her hands to work – by the sweat of her own brow - and draw water daily.

Additionally, to draw water, one would need a vessel to store the water. In the case of a shallow well, a small waterpot or bucket was sufficient. But some wells were so deep that process was more strenuous – involving a much larger bucket and an animal using a pulley-system to draw the water. Because almost every aspect of daily life in ancient Israel involved water (cooking, personal hygiene, farming, tending to livestock, etc.), it was a daily necessity.

Water is synonymous with eternal life, divine revelation and the Holy Spirit. When Jesus met the Samaritan water at the well in John 4, He told her these words: "*Whoever drinks of this water will thirst again, but whoever drinks of the water that I shall give him will never thirst. But the water that I shall give him will become in him a fountain of water springing up into everlasting life.*" This was divine revelation. Jesus was offering the woman an internal well – one from which she could draw from daily. And, if she accepted, the living waters that He promised would become an everlasting well.

> **you will draw water** = with your own hands, by the sweat of your own brow – you will draw divine revelation that will never cease from flowing

from the wells of salvation =

In the interlinear section of the Blue Letter Bible, you'll find that the original word used for 'the wells of salvation' is a feminine noun: *yeshuw'ah*. Strong's definition for '*yeshuw'ah*' is something saved, i.e. deliverance; hence, aid, victory, prosperity.

The Lexicon points to two scripture references: **Psalm 3:3** – "But You, O Lord, are a shield for me, my glory and the One who lifts up my head." And **Psalm 80:3** – "Restore us, O God; cause Your face to shine, and we shall be saved!

> **from the wells of salvation** = a deep well of eternal deliverance, aid victory and prosperity

(E — Envision)

Here is the takeaway from Isaiah 12:3 - Because of the promise of a future and final deliverance - with gladness and rejoicing, you will draw divine revelation from a deep well of eternal deliverance, aid, victory and prosperity.

(D – Declare)

This is my prayer of declaration:

I will draw divine revelation on my own – through my own digging, from my own well. I cannot expect anyone to do the work for me. Just as the 'women of old' would transport their waterpots to the well daily, I must bring my vessel (*my soul – i.e. my mind, my will, and my emotions*) to the well of God's word daily. I declare that divine deliverance, aid, victory and prosperity will flow in abundance in every area of my life. I speak it now and declare that it is so…in Jesus name. Amen!

Week 1

Deborah, Arise

DAY 1

The Right Woman for the Job

Deborah was a woman of extraordinary wisdom and influence who performed the tasks of a judge while the nation of Israel was in turmoil. We meet Deborah in the book of Judges.

Judges 4:1-5

When Ehud was dead, the children of Israel again did evil in the sight of the Lord. ²So the Lord sold them into the hand of Jabin king of Canaan, who reigned in Hazor. The commander of his army was Sisera, who dwelt in Harosheth Hagoyim. ³And the children of Israel cried out to the Lord; for Jabin had nine hundred chariots of iron, and for twenty years he had harshly oppressed the children of Israel.

⁴Now Deborah, a prophetess, the wife of Lapidoth, was judging Israel at that time. ⁵And she would sit under the palm tree of Deborah between Ramah and Bethel in the mountains of Ephraim. And the children of Israel came up to her for judgment.

Let's consider the historical insight:

Israel had been under bondage and oppression for 20 years at the hands of Jabin, the king of Canaan. Because of their own disobedience, the nation was in great despair. Time and time again, the Israelites turned away from God's commands to marry the Canaanites and worship their idol gods (see Judges 2:11-19). As a result, God delivered them into the hands of the surrounding pagan nations. The calamities that the nation faced from their oppressors were designed by God as chastisement that should have lead the people to repentance. Instead, they endured cycles of sin and rebellion for generations. It was during this period that God raised up a judge and prophetess named Deborah, to serve the Israelites in a unique manner. Judges (also known as "Deliverers") guided military expeditions and mediated judicial matters. They were appointed to their leadership roles by God when the deplorable condition of Israel prompted a rescue-plan issued by God Himself.

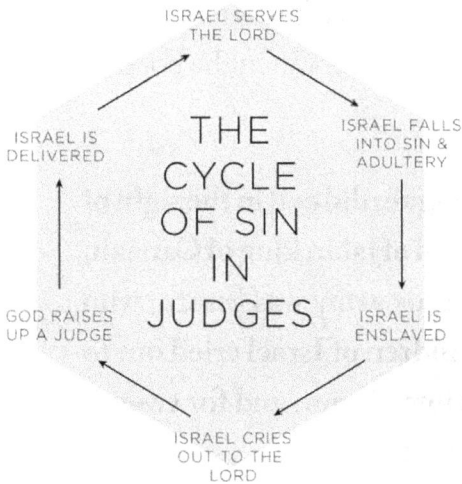

THE CYCLE OF SIN IN JUDGES

ISRAEL SERVES THE LORD
ISRAEL IS DELIVERED
ISRAEL FALLS INTO SIN & ADULTERY
GOD RAISES UP A JUDGE
ISRAEL IS ENSLAVED
ISRAEL CRIES OUT TO THE LORD

The Days of the Judges

Judge	Tribe	Enemy Defeated	Years of	
			Oppression	Rest
Othniel	Judah	Mesopotamia	8 yrs	40 yrs
Ehud	Benjamin	Moabites	18 yrs	80 yrs
Shamgar	?	Philistines	?	?
Deborah	Ephraim	Canaanites	20 yrs	40 yrs
Gideon	Manasseh	Midianites	6 yrs	40 yrs
Tola	Issachar	?		23 yrs
Jair	Manasseh	?		22 yrs
Jephthah	Manasseh	Ammonites	18 yrs	6 yrs
Ibzan	Judah	?		7 yrs
Elon	Zebulon	?		10 yrs
Abdon	Ephraim	?		8 yrs
Samson	Dan	Philistines	40 yrs	20 yrs

2   Hawthorne, Matty. "The Cycle of Sin in Judges." *Ivy Grow Group Blog*, 11 Oct. 2015, https://ivygrowgroups.wordpress.com/2015/10/11/grow-group-notes-11th-17th-october/.

3   "The Days of the Judges." *gegraptai.com*, https://images.app.goo.gl/gKKDKYjXdujnpRAb8. Accessed 23 July 2020.

hy Deborah? Throughout history, God has used uncommon, unpredictable methods to bring about His divine plan. (1 Corinthians 1:27) In this case, He chose to use a woman. Never in the history of Israel's existence had a woman held a position like Deborah's. She was the exception to the rule - breaking rank, defying the odds, shattering the glass ceiling. This was new…different. And, oftentimes, that's exactly where we encounter God.

Dig Deeper

Isaiah 43:19 ESV ~ Behold, I am doing a new thing;
    now it springs forth, do you not perceive it?
I will make a way in the wilderness
    and rivers in the desert.

S — **(Scripture)**

_____

_____

_____

E — **(Examine)**

_____

_____

_____

E — **(Envision)**

_____

_____

_____

D — **(Declare)**

_____

_____

_____

DAY 2

The Grace-Edge

Judges 4:4-5
Now Deborah, a prophetess, the wife of Lapidoth, was judging Israel at that time. ⁵ And she would sit under the palm tree of Deborah between Ramah and Bethel in the mountains of Ephraim. And the children of Israel came up to her for judgment.

Deborah had a 'grace-edge': five keys areas in which she carried out God's divine plan. This 'grace-edge' was a unique anointing that allowed her to operate in her authority with ease. When you are anointed and appointed by God for a specific assignment, His grace makes it look easy. Paul said it best in **1 Corinthians 15:10** ~ 'But by the grace of God I am what I am, and his grace toward me was not in vain. On the contrary, I worked harder than any of them, though it was not I, but the grace of God that is with me.'

The grace of God is the edge - the superior difference-maker. You can wear many hats, but you need His grace. You can be the best to ever do it, but you need His grace. You can be a master multi-tasker, but you need His grace. You can have education, skill and experience, but the grace of God gives you the advantage.

Deborah's "grace-edge"

Prophetess	Judges 4:4	Deborah's first and primary anointing.
Judge	Judges 4:4-5	Deborah epitomized the laws of the land and mediated disputes with justice and order.
Intercessor	Judges 4:5	Deborah took on the role of a spiritual mediator between God and the people.
Military Strategist	Judges 4:6-7	Although she was not a military leader, Deborah worked alongside the leader (Barak) to negotiate a strategy for Israel's victory.
Mother	Judges 5:7	Scripture does not reveal whether Deborah had biological children or not. She embodied this role because of the condition of her people.

Out of all the roles that Deborah would represent, Judges 4:4 introduces her first as a prophetess – *"Now Deborah, a prophetess, the wife of Lapidoth, was judging Israel at that time."*

A prophetess is the feminine expression of a prophet (spokesman or speaker). A prophet, who as motivated by a divine spirit, either rebuked the conduct of kings and nations, or predicted future events. It is understood that prophets (or prophetess') are divine 'mouthpieces' for God. He or she does not speak or operate on their own accord, but are messengers who deliver divine revelation or instruction on God's behalf.

> **If you recognize that you need God's grace for a specific assignment, pause right now and ask Him for it!**
>
> 2 Corinthians 9:8 ~ And God is able to make all grace abound toward you, that you, always having all sufficiency in all things, may have an abundance for every good work.

With that thought in mind, we can establish that Deborah is introduced as a prophetess first, because it is this special prophetic anointing that governs the other roles that God will have her to perform. Deborah was first and primarily God's representative. Her main mission was to hear from God, speak on His behalf, and do His bidding in her region.

The anointing is the foundation of your grace-edge. Vow to never, ever build anything without it.

Dig Deeper

1 John 2:20 ESV ~ But you have been anointed by the Holy One
and you all have knowledge.

S — (Scripture)

_____

_____

_____

E — (Examine)

_____

_____

_____

E — (Envision)

_____

_____

_____

D — (Declare)

_____

_____

_____

DAY 3

Established. Anointed. Sealed. Given.

Anointing = The word is borrowed from a commissioning service that would symbolically set apart kings, prophets, priests, and special servants.[4] In the simplest sense, it is the act of being commissioned by God; empowered with His divine favor and grace; and set apart for His divine service.

The anointing of God was the foundation from which Deborah could build upon. Every other role that she represented was only effective because it had been built and established by the anointing, which was God's seal of approval.

As a believer in Jesus Christ, you too are anointed (*i.e. commissioned by God; empowered with His divine favor and grace; and set apart for His divine service*). The authenticity of a believer is demonstrated by the fact that you are "established", "anointed", "sealed", and "given His Spirit".

---

[4]   MacArthur, John F. *MacArthur Study Bible*, Thomas Nelson, 1997.

2 Corinthians 1:21-22 ~ And it is God who establishes us with you in Christ, and has anointed us, and who has also put his seal on us and given us his Spirit in our hearts as a guarantee.

Established ~ Christ's saving work of grace stabilizes believers and places them on a firm foundation in Him. (Romans 16:25)

Anointed ~ The Holy Spirit sets apart believers and empowers them for the service of gospel proclamation and ministry. (Acts 1:8)

Sealed ~ This refers to the ancient practice of placing soft wax on a document and imprinting the wax with a stamp that indicated ownership, authenticity, and protection. The Holy Spirit attaches all these meanings to His act of spiritually sealing believers. (Ephesians 1:13)

Given ~ God's own Spirit comes to indwell the believer and secures and preserves his eternal salvation. The Holy Spirit is given by God as His pledge of security, authenticity, ownership and authority in the life of the believer. (2 Corinthians 5:5)[5]

When God anoints you, He does it with a purpose in mind. You are not anointed to simply sit on your hands and do nothing. What has God anointed you for? What purpose does your anointing serve? Deborah's anointing was much bigger than the woman - and its purpose much more superior.

What is The Deborah Anointing?

Established, anointed, sealed and given the Holy Spirit to:

- function and flow in and out of roles, responsibilities and relationships
- bring liberation; confronting the powers of darkness with the power of God

---

[5] MacArthur, John F. *MacArthur Study Bible,* Thomas Nelson, 1997.

- be a voice to the voiceless
- pioneer a movement that will empower the next generation to fulfill their God-given destinies
- stand boldly in the call of God, empowered with the grace to lead[6]

[6]   McClain-Walters, Michelle. *The Deborah Anointing: Embracing the Call to be a Woman of Wisdom and Discernment.* Charisma House, 2015.

Dig Deeper

1 Peter 5:10 ESV ~ And after you have suffered a little while, the God of all grace, who has called you to his eternal glory in Christ, will himself restore, confirm, strengthen, and establish you.

S — (Scripture)

_____

_____

_____

E — (Examine)

_____

_____

_____

E — (Envision)

_____

_____

_____

D — (Declare)

_____

_____

_____

DAY 4

Deborah, Arise!

Judges 5:4-7

"Lord, when You went out from Seir,

When You marched from the field of Edom,

The earth trembled and the heavens poured,

The clouds also poured water;

⁵ The mountains gushed before the Lord,

This Sinai, before the Lord God of Israel.

⁶ "In the days of Shamgar, son of Anath,

In the days of Jael,

The highways were deserted,

And the travelers walked along the byways.

Village life ceased, it ceased in Israel,

until I, Deborah, arose, arose a mother in Israel."

Arise = to get up; to rise; to awaken; to come into being, action or notice

There is a distinct call from the Lord during this season for women to arise. You have been anointed for such as time as this. You can no longer keep silent. You can no longer play it safe. Wake up! Arise! Act! Around the globe, women are being mobilized into action like never before. This is the generation where boundaries are being broken, glass ceilings are being shattered, complacency is being challenged, and the silence is being lifted.

Isaiah 60:1-2 ~
Arise, shine, for your light has come, and the glory of the Lord has risen upon you.
For behold, darkness shall cover the earth,
    and thick darkness the peoples;
but the Lord will arise upon you,
    and his glory will be seen upon you.

When did Deborah arise?

- when village life ceased

Village life had ceased. The conditions in Deborah's society had become deplorable and tragic. The will of her people had been broken by the cruelty and ruthlessness of their Canaanite oppressors. They were suffering the consequences of their own disobedience before God. There was a great vacuum of the presence of God in the land. Life had almost come to a standstill. Thieves invaded and caused roads to be abandoned due to the danger of assaults. Trade and commerce had obviously collapsed, for caravans could not even get through the bands of outlaws scattered up and down trade routes. There were no children playing outside, no neighbors standing in the yards engaged in conversations, no socializing in any fashion."[7]

Deborah didn't sit on the sidelines, waiting on someone else to take action. She didn't rally around her girlfriends, complaining about the conditions of the village.

---

[7] McClain-Walters, Michelle. *The Deborah Anointing: Embracing the Call to be a Woman of Wisdom and Discernment.* Charisma House, 2015.

She didn't bury herself under a rock, hoping for the problems to recede. When she realized that the very livelihoods of her people were being threatened and stifled, she had to do something.

Look around you at the state of our world, our nation, and our communities. Many of the world's systems are in turmoil (*educational, political, economical, technological, and even the religion*). Violence, inequality, bigotries, and injustices have become the norm. Self-righteousness is at an all-time high. The lines between right and wrong have been blurred. The very institution of the family is being challenged. The Church has been accused and ridiculed for being out-of-date and out-of-touch. Christians are being lured into this concept of spirituality that is far from a sacred relationship with our heavenly Father. Oh yes, there's trouble in the village for sure.

Remember the infamous quote by the prophet Jeremiah? As a messenger of God, he had been beaten, thrown in prison, threatened, and ridiculed. Although God had put a word in Jeremiah's mouth, the injustice and grievous struggles that he endured were enough to make him quit. Jeremiah became so frustrated that he refused to preach another message…until something was awakened inside him! This intense, internal energy literally felt like fire in his bones.

Jeremiah 20:7-9
O Lord, You induced me, and I was persuaded;
You are stronger than I, and have prevailed.
I am in derision daily;
Everyone mocks me.
⁸ For when I spoke, I cried out;
I shouted, "Violence and plunder!"
Because the word of the Lord was made to me
A reproach and a derision daily.
⁹ Then I said, "I will not make mention of Him,

Nor speak anymore in His name."
But His word was in my heart like a burning fire
Shut up in my bones;
I was weary of holding it back,
And I could not.

Why did Deborah arise?

- she was awakened to the fact that their nation was in "perilous times"
- there was a fire burning inside her and she had no other response except to arise!

Is there a mission burning in your heart? **It's time to arise!**
Is God calling you to do something out of your comfort zone? **It's time to arise!**
Is there a passion that you just can't shake? **It's time to arise!**

Dig Deeper

James 1:17 ESV ~ Every good gift and every perfect gift is from above, coming down from the Father of lights, with whom there is no variation or shadow due to change.

S — (Scripture)

_____

_____

_____

E — (Examine)

_____

_____

_____

E — (Envision)

_____

_____

_____

D — (Declare)

_____

_____

_____

DAY 5

Oh Mother!

Judges 5:6-7
"In the days of Shamgar, son of Anath, in the days of Jael,
the highways were deserted, and the travelers walked along the
byways.
Village life ceased, it ceased in Israel,
until I, Deborah, arose, arose a mother in Israel."

Deborah observed the desolation in Israel and was moved with an urge to bring about deliverance. There was an emptiness in the region that stretched far beyond the deserted fields and the bare highways. For a people, whose culture was built on the backs of their own ability to work, the enemy's oppression was devastating. All commerce had come to a screeching halt; there was no travel on the open highways; there were no caravans of merchants going to and fro. The farmers were driven away from their fields to seek shelter in walled and fenced cities. Thieves and robbers assaulted travelers in the open roads, forcing them to walk in the by-ways as the open roads were no longer safe. These bandits were so bold that no order or decree of government could stop them. War broke out in the courts where justice was usually administered. And the people of Israel had no will to fight at all; in fact, verse 8 proves that *'not a shield or spear was seen among forty thousand in Israel.'* Clearly, this war had been waged against the soul of the Israelites…and Deborah had seen enough.

How did Deborah arise?

* as a mother in Israel (verse 7)
* Mother in Hebrew means "bond", the ability to hold it all together

In the original Hebrew script, the first letter for mother is a picture of an ox. As the ox is strong, the letter also has the meaning of strong. The second letter represents water. The two letters give us the meaning of "strong water." The Hebrews made glue by boiling animal skins in water. As the skin broke down, a sticky thick liquid formed at the surface of the water. This thick liquid was removed and used as a binding agent - "strong water". This is the Hebrew word meaning "mother", the one who "binds" the family together.

Deborah was literally saying: 'I arose as the "strong water / the glue" in Israel. I was given a special anointing by God to hold everything together'. She was the one to do it.

Proverbs 31:29 ~ Many daughters have done well, but you excel them all.
Have you ever had the feeling that you are the one (the glue, the solution, the fighter, the peacemaker)? If so, repeat this affirmation out loud!

Today, I boldly announce that **I am the one**. There is a unique assignment that only I can accomplish. I am the one who will be the catalyst of change for my family. I am the one who will destroy the generational curses. I am the one who will blaze a trail of authenticity with grace and grit. I am the one who will break through so that another woman can break out. I am the one who will open the door for those coming behind me. Today, I take my rightful place as the one. I declare that when I arise - favor, influence and power is rising with me. I am not intimidated or timid... I proudly confess that I am the one! I speak it now and declare that it is so...in Jesus name. Amen!

Dig Deeper

Colossians 1:27 ESV ~ To them God chose to make known how great among the Gentiles are the riches of the glory of this mystery, which is Christ in you, the hope of glory.

S — (Scripture)

_____

_____

_____

E — (Examine)

_____

_____

_____

E — (Envision)

_____

_____

_____

D — (Declare)

_____

_____

_____

Week 2

Deborah, The Honeybee

DAY 1

Deborah - The Honeybee

Deborah's name means "bee". This week, we'll evaluate some key characteristics of the honeybee as we dig into the depths of Deborah's unique anointing. A quick Google search will generate an abundance of information on honeybees. As we study their behaviors and characteristics, we'll parallel Deborah's character to that of a honeybee. With divine wisdom and sovereignty, it is not by accident that God chose a honeybee to deliver Israel!

Because they can maintain a close relationship with humans, the behavior of honeybees has been well-researched. Honeybees live in well-organized colonies and do not require hibernation. They are best known for their production of honey, which they store in wax combs inside nests. Honeybees are generally active during spring, when they go in search of plants from which to collect pollen and nectar. From these two ingredients, they create honey, which humans have harvested for hundreds of years.[8]

---

[8]   "Bee Behavior and Characteristics." *Terminix*, 20 Apr. 2015, https://www.terminix.com/pest-control/bees/behavior/.

Key Characteristics of the Honeybee

Bees produce honey.

A word search in the Blue Letter Bible app (or www.blueletterbible.com) will generate 56 mentions of 'honey' in the King James version. In the original Hebrew language, the word for honey is *debash*, and is defined as a gummy or sticky substance that comes from an unused root. The Proverbs proclaim honey to be *'as sweet as wisdom'*. (Proverbs 24:13-14) Honey is the only food that includes all the substances necessary to sustain life, including enzymes, vitamins, minerals, and water; and it's the only food that contains an antioxidant associated with improving brain function. That's why John the Baptist could survive in the wilderness on locusts and wild honey alone. (Matthew 3:1-4) Honey is more than a sweetener for your hot tea or a condiment for your buttered biscuit.

Have you ever had a 'honey-from-the-rock' encounter with God? Pause right now and think back to a moment when He showed up just in the nick of time. Reflect on how He has provided for you, made a way for you, turned over stones to rescue you, and met you exactly where you needed Him. Think about a time in your life when no one else could get the credit but God. Praise Him for sending resources, wisdom, direction, and clarity from the most unlikely places (like honey from a rock).

It is not by coincidence that the Promised Land flowed with milk & honey. Moses used a metaphor in a song of praise describing how God would *draw honey from the rock* to satisfy the needs of wandering-Israel. (Deuteronomy 32:13, Psalm 81:16) This points to the truth that sometimes the most valuable resources can be found in unlikely places.

When God situated Deborah under the palm tree between Ramah and Bethel in the mountains of Ephraim (Judges 5:5), it was symbolic of a sweet advantage coming to Israel. It was a sign that God would deliver His people from the bitter taste of oppression while healing every single one of their disorders.

Show me the honey!

Proverbs 16:24 ~ Pleasant words are as honeycomb, sweet to the soul, and health to the bones.

Do your lips drip with sweetness or with bitterness? When people encounter you, do they get a sweet or bitter version of you?

Song of Solomon 4:11 ~ Your lips drip nectar, my bride;
honey and milk are under your tongue;
the fragrance of your garments is like the fragrance of Lebanon.

The days of the bitter woman are over. Our words and actions are supposed to bring healing, comfort and peace to the lives of others. If you are struggling to maintain your sweetness; if your words are as sharp as knives; if worry & uncertainty are haunting you; if you are constantly battling with matters in your soul; if the frustrations of life have made you bitter - ask God to heal you. Think about it this way…you have full access to the Creator of the entire universe. There's absolutely nothing too hard for Him. You can go boldly to His throne of grace and ask for what you need. He wants honey to drip from the core of your being.

1 Samuel 14:24-27 ~ And the men of Israel had been hard pressed that day, so Saul had laid an oath on the people, saying, "Cursed be the man who eats food until it is evening and I am avenged on my enemies." So, none of the people had tasted food. [25] Now when all the people came to the forest, behold, there was honey on the ground. [26] And when the people entered the forest, behold, the honey was dripping, but no one put his hand to his mouth, for the people feared the oath. ²⁷ But Jonathan had not heard his father charge the people with the oath, so he put out the tip of the staff that was in his hand and dipped it in the honeycomb and put his hand to his mouth, and his eyes became bright.

Dig Deeper

Psalm 34:8 ESV ~ Oh, taste and see that the Lord is good!
Blessed is the man who takes refuge in him!

S — (Scripture)

_____

_____

_____

E — (Examine)

_____

_____

_____

E — (Envision)

_____

_____

_____

D — (Declare)

_____

_____

_____

DAY 2

Organized Chaos

Bees are creatures of "order" (extremely organized & strategic)

Type of adult bee	What they do	How many in a honey bee colony	How many in a bumble bee colony	What they look like in a honey bee colony	What they look like in a bumble bee colony
Queen	Lay eggs	1	1		
Worker	Take care of larvae, build and clean nest, forage	10,000-50,000	Less than 50 to over 400, depending on species		
Male	Leave nest to mate, then die	100-500	0-50, depending on species and season		

[9]   Huang, Z-Y., and C. Rasmussen."The different types of bees within a colony." *Beespotter*, https://beespotter.org/topics/social/. Accessed 23 July 2020.

Honeybees live in hives (or colonies). The members of the hive are divided into three types:

Queen: One queen runs the whole hive. Her job is to lay the eggs that will spawn the hive's next generation of bees. The queen also produces chemicals that guide the behavior of the other bees.

Workers: These are all female bees and their roles are to hunt for food (pollen and nectar from flowers), build and protect the hive, and clean and circulate air by beating their wings. They are the largest group found in the hive and are responsible for keeping it running smoothly. Workers are the only bees most people ever see flying around outside the hive. Their sense of smell is so precise that it could differentiate hundreds of different floral varieties and tell whether a flower carried pollen or nectar from miles away.

During winter, honeybees feed on the honey they collected during the warmer months. They form a tight cluster in their hive to keep the queen and themselves warm.

Drones: These are the male bees, and their purpose is to mate with the new queen. Several hundred drones live in each hive during the spring and summer. But come winter, when the hive goes into survival mode, the drones are kicked out.

Has your life ever resembled 'organized chaos'? Let's just call it what it is. Jesus never intended for us to organize our chaos. Instead, He compelled us to *"cast every anxiety on Him because He cares for you."* (1 Peter 5:7) Oftentimes, we attach cute and safe adjectives to words and/or behaviors to avoid calling it what it is. If your life is littered with chaos, drama, mess, frustrations, discontentment and despair - cast them on Jesus. To cast means to 'throw something onto something'. So, take this moment right now to gather all your chaos, and throw it as hard and as fast as you can into the capable hands of Jesus.

In the beehive, everyone has a role and responsibility. Worker bees are not trying to compete with the queen bee; they know their roles and perform extremely well. It takes a lot of bees to get all the work done and there is a strategic order to how they work. In fact, the average beehive can have 20,000 to 60,000 bees inside. From the human vantage point, this looks like 'organized chaos'. But the truth is that every single bee in the beehive is carrying their own weight.

God likely had organization and strategy in mind when He appointed Deborah as judge in Israel. He is a God of order. **1 Corinthians 14:40** helps us understand that "all things should be done decently and in order". Deborah's character was perfect for the chaos that was brewing in Israel. Her anointing didn't have to compete or compare with anyone else. Deborah, like the honeybee, was clear about her role. She used her gift to organize and strategize deliverance for her people.

God has designed our lives to be "ordered" like the honeybee. "The steps of a good man are "ordered" by the Lord, and He delights in his way." (Psalm 37:23) The word "ordered" here means established. It is with these same sentiments that David emerged from the chaos to declare in Psalm 40:2 that – "He also brought me up out of a horrible pit, out of the miry clay, and set my feet upon a rock, and established my steps."

Dig Deeper

1 Corinthians 14:33 ESV ~ For God is not a God of confusion but of peace. As in all the churches of the saints,

$\mathcal{S}$ — (Scripture)

_____

_____

_____

$\mathcal{E}$ — (Examine)

_____

_____

_____

$\mathcal{E}$ — (Envision)

_____

_____

_____

$\mathcal{D}$ — (Declare)

_____

_____

_____

DAY 3

Work! Work! Work!

Bees are diligently hard workers.

In the honeybee colony, the workload is always intense. There is never a dull moment. The honeybees work diligently, consistently, and effectively. These social creatures innately understand that their work yields results. They spend their lives performing tasks that benefit the survival of their colony. Although the lifespan of the worker bee is only six weeks or so, they literally work their entire lives. This may be unnerving for some people, because who would ever sign up for 'all work and no play'? One thing is for sure, scripture has a lot to say about work. It is not about how much you work, but the quality and intent of your work is meaningful to God.

Proverbs 12:24 ~ The hand of the diligent will rule, but the lazy man will be put to forced labor.

Proverbs 13:4 ~ The soul of the lazy man desires, and has nothing; but the soul of the diligent shall be made rich.

Psalm 90:17 ~ Let the favor of the Lord our God be upon us, and establish the work of our hands upon us; yes, establish the work of our hands!

Colossians 3:23 ~ Whatever you do, work heartily, as for the Lord and not for men,

1 Corinthians 15:58 ~ Therefore, my beloved brothers, be steadfast, immovable, always abounding in the work of the Lord, knowing that in the Lord your labor is not in vain.

The Deborah (*honeybee*) anointing is synonymous with certain skills and attributes. When we can identify this anointing in our personal lives, these skills are likely unmistakable.

Self-starter, creativity, persistence,
resourcefulness, organization, teachable,
focused, productive, persistent,
responsibility, problem-solving, decisiveness, finishers[10]

Deborah's work ethic was never compromised. She was committed to seeing victory, even if it required her to work overtime.
May God grace you to work the way in which He intended.
May the quality of your work produce impeccable results.
May your diligence pay off in ways that you could only imagine.

---

[10]   McClain-Walters, Michelle. *The Deborah Anointing: Embracing the Call to be a Woman of Wisdom and Discernment.* Charisma House, 2015.

Dig Deeper

2 Timothy 2:15 ESV ~ Do your best to present yourself to God as one approved, a worker who has no need to be ashamed, rightly handling the word of truth.

S — (Scripture)

_____

_____

_____

E — (Examine)

_____

_____

_____

E — (Envision)

_____

_____

_____

D — (Declare)

_____

_____

_____

DAY 4

The Sting of Death

Bees have deadly vengeance.

In addition to working, another task of the honeybee is to protect the colony at all costs. They literally die defending themselves and their colony. Workers in a honeybee hive are the only type of bees with barbed stingers. This means the bee can only sting once. The stinger will lodge itself in the skin of the mammals (including humans), which is fatal to the honeybee when they try to pull away from the victim. Because of this trauma, the bee will die after it has stung, giving its life to protect the hive.

Have you ever been in a fight? We're not talking about a physical fist fight, though you might identify with that as well. We all have private battles we are facing. And there is a real enemy whose primary goal is to steal, kill and destroy you. (John 10:10) There are some battles that are designed to devastate you. There are some battles that will extract everything from you. But what if you knew that you were engaged in a fixed fight? What if you knew that victory was imminent? Would it change the way you fought?

Scripture reminds us that we are constantly at war. (Romans 8:35-39) But don't allow the threat of a battle to deter you. Here's the spoiler alert: you win!

Isaiah 54:17 ~ No weapon formed against you shall prosper,
and every tongue which rises against you in judgment you shall condemn.
This is the heritage of the servants of the Lord
and their righteousness is from me, declares the Lord.

1 Corinthians 15:57 ~ But thanks be to God, who gives
us the victory through our Lord Jesus Christ.

You are equipped. You are well able. You have what it takes. Your situation is not exempt from God's grace. In this human experience, you will face conflicts, disappointment, injustices, uncertainties, etc. But God believes in your victory. He has made it possible for you to triumph in every situation that you will ever encounter.

Many of the battles that we face are not intended to break us, but instead they are building something eternal on the inside of us.

Like the honeybee, you have an internal 'stinger'. When danger lurks, your God-instinct is to protect your hive and attack when necessary. Never make apologies for the fighter inside you. God designed you that way. "You are of God, little children, and have overcome them, because He who is in you is greater than he who is in the world." (1 John 4:4)

This is why Deborah's story is so unique. Because of her 'honeybee' qualities, she was a natural-born fighter. Amid national distress,

If you are currently engaged in a battle that is smothering the life out of you, it's time to activate your 'internal stinger'. Issue a sting of death to every force that is opposing you, to every voice that is trying to silence you and to every weight that is trying to break you. Push back the darkness with prayer, fasting and daily declarations from the Word.

Deborah devised a plan to seek vengeance for the people of Israel. She summoned a man named Barak from Kedesh-Naphtali and commanded him to 'Go and deploy troops…' (Judges 4:6) Deborah's plea for Barak to join her activated an entire army toward her cause.

You are not alone. Who have you invited into battle with you?

Judges 4:6-9

She sent and summoned Barak the son of Abinoam from Kedesh-naphtali and said to him, "Has not the Lord, the God of Israel, commanded you, 'Go, gather your men at Mount Tabor, taking 10,000 from the people of Naphtali and the people of Zebulun. 7 And I will draw out Sisera, the general of Jabin's army, to meet you by the river Kishon with his chariots and his troops, and I will give him into your hand'?" 8 Barak said to her, "If you will go with me, I will go, but if you will not go with me, I will not go." 9 And she said, "I will surely go with you. Nevertheless, the road on which you are going will not lead to your glory, for the Lord will sell Sisera into the hand of a woman."

Dig Deeper

2 Corinthians 2:14 ESV ~ But thanks be to God, who in Christ always leads us in triumphal procession, and through us spreads the fragrance of the knowledge of him everywhere.

S — (Scripture)

_____

_____

_____

E — (Examine)

_____

_____

_____

E — (Envision)

_____

_____

_____

D — (Declare)

_____

_____

_____

DAY 5

You'll Never Run Dry

Bees operate in unity.

> **Romans 14:19 ~ So then let us pursue what makes for peace and for mutual up-building.**

> **1 Corinthians 14:12 ~ So with yourselves, since you are eager for manifestations of the Spirit, strive to excel in building up the church.**

It is a known fact that honey bees can sometimes visit up to 2,000 flowers in a day. When a honey bee finds a good source of nectar, she flies back to the colony and shows her fellow bees where the nectar source is by dancing. According to bee experts, the honey bee dance plays an important role in the survival of the species and has been a part of colonies for centuries. The honey bee dance is the most effective way for bees to communicate with one another. A honey bee that discovers a new food source will tell other honey bees about its location through the dance. When a worker bee returns from an abundant food source, she will dance inside their nest in a circle.

There are no secrets in the colony. Everything the honey bee learns or finds, she brings back to the colony.

What is it that you know that you can share? What tools, strategies and insights have God downloaded to your spirit? Bring them back to the colony so someone else can benefit from what He has given you.

Can you tell someone how you manifested your breakthrough?

How you shed the guilt from your past?

How you got over or mended a broken relationship?

How you released your fears and began walking in your faith?

How you lost the weight, got through the grief, raised the children, served an aging parent, got the promotion, started the business – share it!

There is a colony of women who need you. Your skills, your wisdom, your experiences, your ideas, your creativity, your story matters – and it is needed now more than ever.

When you pour from yourself, out of obedience to God, you'll never be depleted. Remember the story of the widow woman's oil in 2 Kings 4? This woman cried out to the prophet Elisha saying that her husband was dead, and the creditors had come to take her sons. Elisha asked her "*what do you have in your house?*" She said, "I have nothing in the house but a jar of oil". Elisha instructed her to go and borrow vessels from her neighbors - as many as she could find. She followed his instructions, and returned home to pour into those borrowed vessels until they were all filled. As long as she had vessels, the oil flowed. When there were no more vessels, the oil ceased.

The moral of the story? You are the vessel.

If you are willing to pour from yourself into another vessel…

the oil of God's anointing will flow,

resources will come in abundance,

health and healing will be your portion,

peace will be made available to you,

and you'll never run dry…in Jesus name!

Dig Deeper

2 Corinthians 4:7 ESV ~ But we have this treasure in jars of clay, to show that the surpassing power belongs to God and not to us.

S — (Scripture)

_____

_____

_____

E — (Examine)

_____

_____

_____

E — (Envision)

_____

_____

_____

D — (Declare)

_____

_____

_____

Week 3

Deborah, The Worshiping Warrior

DAY 1

Deborah - The Worshiping Warrior

Psalm 144:1 ~ "Blessed be the Lord my Rock, who trains my hands for war, and my fingers for battle."

Based on our study from last week, we have a better understanding of Deborah, the honeybee. If we reconciled everything that her name represents, we would find that there is great substance and depth at the core of who Deborah was. Because of her namesake, we can ascertain that Deborah was sweet yet powerful, extremely organized, a strategic thought leader, diligent in her work, and a unified force to be reckoned.

This week, we are diving into the heart of Deborah's anointing. We will explore how she used worship as an antidote on the battlefield. As women, we cannot make the mistake of limiting worship to a tearful melody sang with closed eyes and uplifted hands. Worship is multi-faceted - and it is undeniably one of your greatest weapons.

The dictionary defines worship as the reverent love and devotion expressed to a deity, an idol or a sacred object. It is also defined as the ceremonies, prayers or other religious forms by which this love is expressed. If you type 'worship' in the Topical Bible section of OpenBible.info, you'll find the top 100 scriptures pertaining to worship. Clearly, the Bible has a lot to say about worship, and we should be listening with all ears.

The root word for worship is *shachah*, meaning to bow down. When the Samaritan woman encountered Jesus at the well, He told her *"You worship what you do not know; we know what we worship, for salvation is of the Jews. But the hour is coming, and now is, when the true worshipers will worship the Father in spirit and truth; for the Father is seeking such to worship Him. God is Spirit, and those who worship Him must worship in spirit and truth."* (John 4:22-24) Jesus was pointing to the fact that our worship is not simply an outward religious ritual, but an inward (*in spirit*) conviction of the heart given to the True and Living God (*in truth*). Everything in our lives – who we are, who we hope to be - must bow down in complete surrender to God. And this, my friend, is what makes worship so powerful.

Deborah held worship in such high regard that she dedicated the entire chapter of Judges 5 to praise and worship. We will call her the worshiping warrior because she bowed down in worship despite her title and position in Israel. Deborah and Barak sang a song of victory highlighting how God had gone before them in battle and guaranteed their victory. We'll get to the actual battle soon, but it's quite possible that Deborah penned the lyrics to her song of worship before the soldiers even stepped onto the battlefield.

Judges 5:1 ~ Then Deborah and Barak the son of Abinoam sang on that day...

Deborah, the prophetess, knew that victory was imminent. Perhaps her song was a foreshadow of the same sort of victory that God guaranteed Jehoshaphat centuries later in 2 Chronicles 20:17. *"You will not need to fight in this battle. Position yourselves, stand still and see the salvation of the Lord, who is with you, O Judah and Jerusalem! Do not fear or be dismayed; tomorrow go out against them, for the Lord is with you."*

So, on that day, Deborah and Barak sang a song that had already been written. Why? Because you don't wait until the battle is won to praise and worship the Lord. You, like Deborah, will usher in the victory through your worship.

2 Chronicles 20:22

"Believe in the Lord your God, so shall ye be established; believe His prophets, so shall ye prosper. And when he had consulted with the people, he appointed singers unto the Lord, and that should praise the beauty of holiness, as they went out before the army, and to say, Praise the Lord; for his mercy endures forever. And when they began to sing and to praise, the Lord set ambushments against the (enemy) and they were smitten,"

Dig Deeper

Colossians 3:16 ESV ~ Let the word of Christ dwell in you richly, teaching and admonishing one another in all wisdom, singing psalms and hymns and spiritual songs, with thankfulness in your hearts to God.

S — (Scripture)

_____

_____

_____

E — (Examine)

_____

_____

_____

E — (Envision)

_____

_____

_____

D — (Declare)

_____

_____

_____

DAY 2

Your Words Have Power

Psalm 19:14 ~ Let the words of my mouth and the meditation of my heart be acceptable in your sight, O Lord, my rock and my redeemer.

Words matter. Your words matter. What you say can either help or hinder you. How you define your life is evident in the words that you speak.

Never underestimate the power of your words. The success of your family, business, ministry, marriage, life, etc. is in your mouth. Likewise, the failure of your life also hinges on your spoken word. Words are so powerful that scripture warns us that we will give an account for idle (useless, lazy, barren) words at the day of judgement (Matthew 12:36). The very essence of what your life will become is a result of the words you speak.

Make no mistake, your words also have creative power. God created the entire universe with 3 words, "let there be". As a believer, you have the authority to give good things permission to exist in your life. What will you create with your words?

You can change your life, one word at a time.

Judges 4:14 ~ *Then Deborah said to Barak, "Up! For this is the day in which the Lord has delivered Sisera into your hand. "Has not the Lord gone out before you?" So Barak went down from Mount Tabor with ten thousand men following him.*

Deborah opened her prophetic announcement with one powerful word: Up! The Bible doesn't explain why she chose to say "Up", but we can ascertain that she intended to move Barak and his army to action. Were they sitting still, wallowing in their sorrows, having pity on themselves, afraid to move? We don't know. But what we do know is that when a woman says "Up!", she means exactly what she said. Get up! Look Up! Rise Up! Show Up! And don't you dare delay.

Who or what can stop a woman with a made-up mind? She is like a freight train running with no brakes. When you change your mind, your words will soon follow. When you change the words that you speak, the game changes. Today, repeat this affirmation out loud.

Today, I boldly confess that I have what it takes to change the game. By faith, I am an overcomer. By faith, I am victorious. By faith, I can do the impossible. How do I change the game? I do this by changing my mind. Therefore, I change my mind about being at the bottom…I declare that I'm going to the top. I change my mind about being behind…I declare that I'm coming to the front. I change my mind about not having enough…I declare that I will live in abundance. I change my mind about being inadequate…I declare that I can do all things. I declare that I will overcome every obstacle, break through every boundary, shatter every limitation, destroy every hindrance, and conquer every challenge. When I change the game, nothing will be able to contain me. In Jesus name. Amen!

Dig Deeper

Psalm 141:3 ESV ~ Set a guard, O Lord, over my mouth;
keep watch over the door of my lips!

S — (Scripture)

_____

_____

_____

E — (Examine)

_____

_____

_____

E — (Envision)

_____

_____

_____

D — (Declare)

_____

_____

_____

DAY 3

Worship in the Wilderness

Psalm 63:1 ~ O God, You are my God; early will I seek You; my flesh longs for You in a dry and thirsty land where there is no water.

David wrote this psalm while hiding in the wilderness of Judea (2 Samuel 15:23), but longing to be back worshiping in Jerusalem. Absalom, his son, betrayed King David by forming a conspiracy to steal the hearts of the people and essentially the throne. David, not sure how far Absolom was willing to go, feared for his life and went into hiding. Although he found himself in the wilderness - scared and uncertain of the future - David never lost his worship. The wilderness can be understood as a place of isolation, oftentimes dark, stony and void of vegetation.

Even as a bible-believing, faith-filled Christian, you can sometimes find yourself in the wilderness. Whether it's just for a night or you've been there for an extended period, the wilderness can leave you desperate, lonely, afflicted, confused, frustrated and unsettled.

But there's a different kind of worship that is born in the wilderness. It often starts as a tearful, fretful plea that turns into the purest form of self-sacrifice. Worship, especially from the wilderness, is sacred. It is the kind of worship that forgets the fact that you may be facing a severe divine drought, or a devastating loss, or a gut-wrenching blow to your sanity. Your cries from the wilderness are a sweet aroma to our God. Choose to worship. And when you do, you'll resemble the words and heart-worship of Deborah in Judges 5:3. *"Hear, O kings! Give ear, O princes! I, even I, will sing to the Lord; I will sing praise to the Lord God of Israel."*

I, even I – with my wilderness still in the rearview mirror – will sing a song of worship to my God!

Deborah's proclamation to sing is echoed by the words of David in Psalm 27:6. *"And now my head shall be lifted up above my enemies all around me; therefore, I will offer sacrifices of joy in His tabernacle; I will sing, yes, I will sing praises to the Lord."* This psalm depicts the strong contrasts that we will experience in our Christian journey - lament and laud; persecution and praise; warfare and worship. It is also an indication that regardless of the circumstances of life, worship is eternally essential.

Dig Deeper

Psalm 62:5 ESV ~ For God alone, O my soul, wait in silence, for my hope is from him.

S — (Scripture)

_____

_____

_____

E — (Examine)

_____

_____

_____

E — (Envision)

_____

_____

_____

D — (Declare)

_____

_____

_____

DAY 4

The Watering Places

Judges 5:7-11

Village life ceased, it ceased in Israel,

Until I, Deborah, arose,

Arose a mother in Israel.

⁸ They chose new gods;

Then *there was* war in the gates;

Not a shield or spear was seen among forty thousand in Israel.

⁹ My heart *is* with the rulers of Israel

Who offered themselves willingly with the people.

Bless the Lord!

¹⁰ "Speak, you who ride on white donkeys,

Who sit in judges' attire,

And who walk along the road.

¹¹ Far from the noise of the archers, among the watering places,

There they shall recount the righteous acts of the Lord,

The righteous acts *for* His villagers in Israel;

Then the people of the Lord shall go down to the gates.

Deborah paints a vivid picture of the turmoil and distress that the Israelites were under. She acknowledges that they had taken matters into their own hands: *'They chose new gods'*. They had grown tired of waiting on the Lord to rescue them. The misery, anxiety, uncertainty, and mayhem that they were facing was a result of their own doing. Their God, who is the Ancient of Days, will never fail them – not yesterday, not today, not ever. But His people wanted gods of their own choosing. And their idolatry is what provoked God to turn the Israelites into the hands of their enemies.

In her poetic song, Deborah points to the fact that *'there was war in the gates, and not a shield or spear was seen among forty thousand in Israel'*; meaning that the conditions were so bad and morale was so low, that the Israelites didn't even bother to bring weapons to the battle. Deborah addresses all the people, regardless of their background. She called for those 'who ride on white donkeys', those 'who sit on rich carpets', and those 'who walk by the way.' Rich, poor or indifferent. They were all invited to join the musicians at 'the watering places.'

Let's pause here for a moment.
If Deborah and Barak were preparing the nation for battle, why was it necessary to make a pit stop by 'the watering places'?

One word: Repentance.

The words of Peter from Acts 3:19 hold true for this moment. *"Repent therefore and be converted, that your sins may be blotted out, so that times of refreshing may come from the presence of the Lord."*

The Greek word for 'refreshing' signifies any kind of refreshing, as a rest, renewal or deliverance from evils of any kind. The Israelites were surely in need of a refreshing, which is why Deborah compelled them to meet her at the watering places. These dug-out wells were typically set in a remote distance from the towns. During times of peace they were a place of rest and refuge for residents and travelers alike. But during times of conflict and social unrest, the wells were a dangerous place to be. Yet, it was a necessary layover.

When Jesus and the woman at the well engaged in dialogue, He told her that *"whoever drinks of this water will thirst again, but whoever drinks of the water that I shall give him will never thirst. But the water that I shall give him will become in him a fountain of water springing up into everlasting life."* (John 4:13-14) And He sat upon that watering place and told her the meaning of true worship.

The watering places are necessary. It is where we repent. It is where we lay down our sin and wrong-doing. It is where we give up our privilege, and self-righteousness, and self-dependence, and idolatry, and immorality. It is where we can come empty-handed, heart-broken, fully-depleted. And it is where God – and God alone - refreshes us.

Dig Deeper

Psalm 51:7 ESV ~ Purge me with hyssop, and I shall be clean; wash me, and I shall be whiter than snow.

S — (Scripture)

_____

_____

_____

E — (Examine)

_____

_____

_____

E — (Envision)

_____

_____

_____

D — (Declare)

_____

_____

_____

DAY 5

Wake Up The Morning

Judges 5:12 ~ "Awake, awake, Deborah!
Awake, awake, break out in a song!
Arise, Barak, lead away your captives,
O son of Abinoam.

Awake means to rouse from sleep, to make aware of, to stir up, to become aware or alert.

Deborah's song is Judges 5 is an awakening plea, not only to herself, but also to the troops who were going into battle. Her intention is to stir up worship in such a way that their voices are heard all the way to the frontlines. Deborah repeats the words 'awake, awake' as if she was literally trying to shake herself at the very core. Make a mental note that Deborah addresses herself first and then Barak. Perhaps this is because you can't expect someone to do something that you are not willing to do yourself. Awake! Arise!

True worship has a way of unlocking the relentless warrior inside of you. Not only does it bring you into the presence of the Lord, but it changes your perspective. When we worship, we shift our focus off our circumstances and onto our God. So, when Deborah – the Mother of Israel - cried out *'awake, awake, break out in a song'*, she was inviting her fellow warriors to shift the atmosphere alongside her. Awake! Arise!

In the same manner, David repeated similar sentiments in Psalms 57:8 and 108:2. He spoke to himself first and then to the dawn.

"Awake, my glory! Awake, lute and harp! I will awaken the dawn."
Psalm 57:8

"Awake, lute and harp! I will awaken the dawn."
Psalms 108:2

David's intention was to stir up the morning. In a sense, he was saying to the morning: "Get up! You've been asleep long enough. I've seen the darkness of night for far too long, wake up!" David refused to wait until morning to worship the Lord. Instead, he commenced to worship in such a way that not even the sun could resist rising – not even the dew could hold its vapor – and morning couldn't sleep any longer. In Psalm 57:8, David called for his glory to be awakened. The word 'glory' is referring to the core of the man; the rational, intellectual, emotional part of his being; his soul (mind, will and emotions). If you are going to wake up the morning, you'd better know how to ask God to silence the worries in your

How can one possibly wake up morning?

You do it with your worship – pure, unrestrained, sincere worship. The heart of God is keen on worship. It is a sweet aroma in His nostrils, like the sacrificial death of Christ. (2 Corinthians 2:15) Worship smells like death burning on an altar – death to your will and your way.

Today, surrender to the heaviness of God's presence in worship. Allow your words to become like a thick cloud of smoke that reaches the altar of God.

mind, to break your will until it aligns with His will, and to put your emotions at ease. This type of humility is at the heart of worship.

David continues with these words in Psalm 57: *"I will praise You, O Lord, among the peoples; I will sing to You among the nations. For Your mercy reaches unto the heavens, and Your truth unto the clouds. Be exalted, O God, above the heavens; let Your glory be above all the earth."*

God's mercy, truth and glory are incomprehensible. His grandeur and majesty are beyond words. His wisdom exceeds our logic and reasoning. The extent of His power, love, patience and faithfulness is inexhaustible. And for this, we should forever worship Him.

Dig Deeper

Psalm 30:5 ESV ~ For his anger is but for a moment,
   and his favor is for a lifetime.
Weeping may tarry for the night,
   but joy comes with the morning.

S — (Scripture)

_____

_____

_____

E — (Examine)

_____

_____

_____

E — (Envision)

_____

_____

_____

D — (Declare)

_____

_____

_____

Week 4

The Queen of Breakthrough

DAY 1

The Tent Woman

Judges 4:14-17 ~

Then Deborah said to Barak, "Up! For this *is* the day in which the Lord has delivered Sisera into your hand. Has not the Lord gone out before you?" So Barak went down from Mount Tabor with ten thousand men following him. And the Lord routed Sisera and all *his* chariots and all *his* army with the edge of the sword before Barak; and Sisera alighted from *his* chariot and fled away on foot. But Barak pursued the chariots and the army as far as Harosheth Hagoyim, and all the army of Sisera fell by the edge of the sword; not a man was left.

However, Sisera had fled away on foot to the tent of Jael, the wife of Heber the Kenite; for *there was* peace between Jabin king of Hazor and the house of Heber the Kenite.

The enemy had mobilized a massive army against the Israelites, but the victory was already spoken for. Remember the prophetic words of Deborah in Judges 4:9? She told Barak, *"I will surely go with you (into battle); nevertheless, there will be no glory for you in the journey you are taking, for the Lord will sell Sisera into the hand of a woman."*

And this is where the tent woman, Jael, enters the story.

Sisera, Captain of Jabin's army, slipped off his horse and ran as fast as he could away from the destruction. His entire army had been annihilated and Sisera was looking for a safe place to hide out. He entered the tent of Jael, the wife of Heber, who was at peace with his boss Jabin. In accordance with the customs of that time, Jael greeted Sisera with warm hospitality, offering refreshments and giving him a comfortable place to rest. We don't know what her intention was – whether she was driven by instinct or whether she knew that she was an instrument in the hand of God. Jael took a tent peg and a hammer into her hand – and with one courageous blow, she drove the tent peg through Sisera's temple and fastened it securely into the ground. And the enemy of Israel died on the floor of a tent woman.

> Jael was a fierce, yet ordinary warrior who rose to the call of action. Isaiah 60:1 says *"arise, shine, for your light has come, and the glory of the Lord has risen upon you."* Yes, you! Arise! Shine!
>
> What are you going to do when God's spotlight of glory shines upon you?
> What are you going to do when the Lord presents an opportunity to be used for His glory?
> Will you be prepared to step up to the challenge?
> Will you shrink back in fear?
> Or will you break free of every limitation and seize the moment to bring the Lord glory?
>
> That's exactly what Jael did. She turned her tent into a battleground and secured her place in history.

Dig Deeper

Isaiah 45:3 ESV ~ I will give you the treasures of darkness
    and the hoards in secret places,
that you may know that it is I, the Lord,
    the God of Israel, who call you by your name.

S — (Scripture)

_____

_____

_____

E — (Examine)

_____

_____

_____

E — (Envision)

_____

_____

_____

D — (Declare)

_____

_____

_____

DAY 2

It's Moving Day

Judges 4:11 ~ Now Heber the Kenite, of the children of Hodab the father-in-law of Moses, had separated himself from the Kenites and pitched his tent near the terebinth tree at Zaanaim, which is beside Kedesh.

Heber, Jael's husband, had separated himself from his people (the Kenites) and moved their tent away from the battlefield. The reason for his moving is not mentioned in scripture, but we see God involved in the decision. Later on, when Sisera is running away from the war, the location of Heber & Jael's tent plays a major role in the story. "However, Sisera had fled away on foot to the tent of Jael, the wife of Heber the Kenite. (Judges 4:17) And this is where we witness a strategic trait of God's character – His providence.

Providence is defined as foresight or divine direction. It is the foreseeing care, thoughtful planning and meticulous guidance of God toward His creation. We see the providential hand of God echoed throughout the scriptures.

Proverbs 16:9 ~ The heart of man plans his way, but the Lord establishes his steps.

Proverbs 16:33 ~ The lot is cast into the lap, but its ever decision is from the Lord.

Jeremiah 29:11 ~ For I know the plans I have for you, declares the Lord, plans for welfare and not for evil, to give you a future and a hope.

Romans 8:28 ~ And we know that for those who love God all things work together for good, for those who are called according to His purpose.

It is not by coincidence that Heber & Jael uprooted their tent and pitched it near the terebinth tree near Kedesh. They had no way of knowing that Sisera would need a place to hide out, but God did. He is constantly and eternally involved in the details of our affairs. Just when you think that God has forgotten you, or He's not aware of the nuances of your life – He sees you. Who you are - and who you're becoming - is all a part of His divine plan. And, whether you know it or not, His providential hand is always at work.

Psalm 139:1-6
O Lord, You have searched me and known me. You know my sitting down and my rising up;
You understand my thought afar off. You comprehend my path and my lying down,
And are acquainted with all my ways. For there is not a word on my tongue,
But behold, O Lord, You know it altogether. You have hedged me behind and before,
And laid Your hand upon me. Such knowledge is too wonderful for me;
It is high, I cannot attain it.

Today is moving day! Center yourself in perfect alignment with God's plan and purpose for your life. At the end of Psalm 139, after David praised God for His knowing him down to the smallest detail, he prayed – "search me, O God, and know my heart; try me and know my anxieties; and see if there is any wicked way in me, and lead me in the way everlasting." This is a prayer of alignment – one that offers routine maintenance on your very soul.

Jael was in direct alignment with God's providential plan. Her internal instinct, who she was married to, the location of her tent, the timing of their move – it all aligned at the right moment. Accept this truth: nothing and no one can stop a woman who is in divine alignment with her God.

Dig Deeper

Psalm 139:14 ESV ~ I will praise You, for I am fearfully and wonderfully made. Wonderful are your works; my soul knows it very well.

S — (Scripture)

_____

_____

_____

E — (Examine)

_____

_____

_____

E — (Envision)

_____

_____

_____

D — (Declare)

_____

_____

_____

DAY 3

The Beauty and the Beast

Judges 5:24-27 ~
"Most blessed among women is Jael,
The wife of Heber the Kenite;
Blessed is she among women in tents.
He asked for water, she gave milk;
She brought out cream in a lordly bowl.
She stretched her hand to the tent peg,
Her right hand to the workmen's hammer;
She pounded Sisera, she pierced his head,
She split and struck through his temple.
At her feet he sank, he fell, he lay still;
At her feet he sank, he fell;
Where he sank, there he fell dead.

What would you do if you were face-to-face with the enemy? How would you respond if he slipped inside your dwelling place? What actions would you take if given the opportunity?

The Bible is clear - you have an enemy. One who is a cunning, deceitful liar. Satan is God's adversary, which makes him your adversary as well.

The scriptures depict Satan as a fallen angel who rebelled against God. (Luke 10:18) The demons mentioned throughout the scriptures are evil spirits whose job is to do Satan's dirty work on earth. These beings are described as fallen angels lured away from heaven by the devil himself. (Revelations 12:4) Throughout the gospels, demons not only knew Jesus' true identity, but they trembled before His authority as God.

Satan's greatest advantage is that many people do not believe he exists. Over the centuries, he has been portrayed as a caricature with horns, a spiked tail and a pitchfork. However, Jesus knew exactly who Satan was and didn't cower when it came to his final destiny. (John 8:44, Romans 16:20, Colossians 2:14-15, Revelation 12:10)

Satan and all his companions are already defeated through the death, burial and resurrection of Jesus Christ. Their ultimate destruction is imminent. However, these forces of darkness will continue to oppose and antagonize those who believe in Jesus. But don't you dare allow the thought and threat of your enemy to chase you into corner. You are powerful beyond measure – never forget it. Remind yourself of who you are. Through Jesus Christ,

you are victorious (1 Corinthians 15:57)

you are forgiven (Ephesians 4:32)

you are free (John 8:36)

you are blessed (Ephesians 1:3)

you are loved (Romans 8:38-39)

you are strong (Philippians 4:13)

you are redeemed (Galatians 3:13)

you are chosen (1 Peter 2:9)

you are complete (Colossians 2:10)

you are the light of the world (Matthew 5:14-16)

Sisera represented a beast that had to be defeated. He and his goons had troubled the Israelites for long enough. And when Jael was face-to-face with the enemy, she didn't back down. She didn't even talk. She took matters into her own hands – literally. With power and precision, Jael silenced the enemy once and for all.

This battle – the one you and I are in – will require a different set of weapons. Jael used a tent peg and hammer. We have been commissioned by the Word to fight differently. We fight on our knees in prayer - using the Word against every evil force that opposes us. In Ephesians 6, Paul gives a vivid description of the spiritual outfit that Christians should wear daily. We are to cloth ourselves with the garments of truth, righteousness and peace. And we are to arm ourselves with faith, the assurance of our salvation, and the Word of God. And make no mistake about it, when you wear the proper armor, you may win the battle but God will ultimately win the war.

> *Ephesians 6:10-17 ~ Finally, my brethren, be strong in the Lord and in the power of His might. ¹¹ Put on the whole armor of God, that you may be able to stand against the wiles of the devil. ¹² For we do not wrestle against flesh and blood, but against principalities, against powers, against the rulers of the darkness of this age, against spiritual hosts of wickedness in the heavenly places. ¹³ Therefore take up the whole armor of God, that you may be able to withstand in the evil day, and having done all, to stand.*
>
> *¹⁴ Stand therefore, having girded your waist with truth, having put on the breastplate of righteousness, ¹⁵ and having shod your feet with the preparation of the gospel of peace; ¹⁶ above all, taking the shield of faith with which you will be able to quench all the fiery darts of the wicked one. ¹⁷ And take the helmet of salvation, and the sword of the Spirit, which is the word of God;*

Dig Deeper

James 4:7 ESV ~ Submit yourselves therefore to God. Resist the devil, and he will flee from you.

S — (Scripture)

_____

_____

_____

E — (Examine)

_____

_____

_____

E — (Envision)

_____

_____

_____

D — (Declare)

_____

_____

_____

DAY 4

The Breakthrough Strategy

The Bible doesn't give us a lot of details about Jael. All we know is that her name is Jael and she was the wife of Heber, the Kenite. Through a quick search on Blue Letter Bible, you'll find that her Hebrew name was *Ya'el* which means mountain goat. Oftentimes when you don't have all the details about a biblical person, digging into the little information that is provided can help to paint a better picture of who they were. Many biblical names, for example, were rich in symbolism and carried great significance. A name in the Bible can indicate a person's origin, purpose, traits and characteristics. As you study the scriptures, pay attention to specifics such as names, locations/geography and lineage. These facts can sometimes help you understand the context and overall meaning of the scriptures.

With her name in mind – Jael (the mountain goat), let's unpack more about her character. A Wikipedia search reveals that mountain goat's feet are well-suited for climbing steep, rocky slopes. They are related to antelopes and gazelles based on their anatomy. The tips of their feet have sharp dewclaws that keep them from slipping. And mountain goats have powerful shoulder and neck muscles that help propel them up steep slopes. Beautiful - but rugged. Swift - but graceful. Why is this important? Because Jael was hand-picked to carry out an assignment that was tailor-made for her.

In Deborah's song, she highlighted where Sisera fell – at Jael's feet. *"At her feet he sank, he fell, he lay still; at her feet he sank, he fell; where he sank, there he fell dead."* (Judges 5:27) That's the image you can't overlook. The enemy fell at her feet, just as he should have. In one of the most prophetic portions of scripture, David exclaimed that *"The Lord said to my Lord, 'Sit at My right hand, till I make Your enemies Your footstool."* (Psalm 110:1) This is a foreshadow of Jesus sitting at the right hand of the Father with absolute and eternal victory – and the enemy is under His feet. Jesus has given you *"'the authority to trample on serpents and scorpions, and over all the power of the enemy, and nothing shall by any means hurt you."* (Luke 10:10)

Jael was a simple, ordinary woman dwelling in tents amongst her people. This suggests that she didn't have a permanent dwelling, which is symbolic of life in the wilderness. Some may have seen her as insignificant in comparison to the anointed, powerful Deborah. Although she didn't carry the same responsibility as Deborah, she was anointed nonetheless. But, regardless of our background and history, there is a place on the battlefield for each of us!

Here's 3 things we learn from Jael's actions:

1) Jael was alone when she faced the greatest enemy of her lifetime.

- Your most intense battles usually happen when you're alone.

Ephesians 6:12 - For we do not wrestle against flesh and blood, but against principalities, against powers, against the rulers of the darkness of this age, against spiritual hosts of wickedness in the heavenly places.

- For every silent battle you face, you have the victory!
- For every whisper from the enemy, you have the victory!
- For every intimidation and fear, you have the victory!
- For every deceptive lie, you have the victory!
- For every secret struggle, you have the victory!

2) Jael used what was in her hands.

- What has God put in your hands? What gifts? Talents? Skills? Resources? Ideas? In your hands, it may seem insignificant. But in the hands of our Mighty God, it can be everything.

Exodus 4:2 – So the Lord said to him (Moses), "What is that in your hand?" He said, "A rod."

Jael used her hands to finish what Deborah started - and guaranteed 40 years of peace for the people of Israel.

3) God used Jael as a strategy for breakthrough.

God interrupted the life of an ordinary woman and deployed her as a strategy against the enemy. Can you receive that for yourself today? YOU are the strategy. You are the secret weapon. You are the one. Who you are - what you possess - the experiences that you've had - the lessons you've learned - God can use it.

Here's the key: the woman in the tent and the woman on the frontline both received the same reward…breakthrough!

Dig Deeper

John 8:32 ESV ~ and you will know the truth,
and the truth will set you free."

S — **(Scripture)**

_____

_____

_____

E — **(Examine)**

_____

_____

_____

E — **(Envision)**

_____

_____

_____

D — **(Declare)**

_____

_____

_____

DAY 5

Woman, Arise

Breakthrough = a significant or sudden advancement; the act of overcoming or penetrating an obstacle or restriction; a major achievement or success that permits further progress.[11]

> **Psalm 18:28-36**
> **For You will light my lamp;**
> **The Lord my God will enlighten my darkness.**
> **[29] For by You I can run against a troop,**
> **By my God I can leap over a wall.**
> **[30] *As for* God, His way *is* perfect;**
> **The word of the Lord is proven;**
> **He *is* a shield to all who trust in Him.**
> **[31] For who *is* God, except the Lord?**
> **And who *is* a rock, except our God?**
> **[32] *It is* God who arms me with strength,**
> **And makes my way perfect.**

---

11 "Breakthrough." *Dictionary.com*, 2020, https://www.dictionary.com/browse/breakthrough.

³³ **He makes my feet like the *feet of* deer,**

And sets me on my high places.

³⁴ **He teaches my hands to make war,**

So that my arms can bend a bow of bronze.

³⁵ **You have also given me the shield of Your salvation;**

Your right hand has held me up,

Your gentleness has made me great.

³⁶ **You enlarged my path under me,**

So my feet did not slip.

Throughout this study, we've been doing a beautiful dance between the words, songs and praises of Deborah and David. In Psalm 18, David sings a song of thanksgiving to summarize the testimony of his entire life. The Bible does not specifically use the word 'breakthrough', but David gives us a picture of what it looks like. Here are some truths that we can glean from his testimony:

- God will cause your inner light to shine – and He will illuminate every area of darkness in your life.
- God will give you the ability to run through crowds and leap over high walls. Nothing will be able to stop you.
- God will equip your feet to stand firmly in times of testing and trouble – and He will set you securely in high places.
- God will train you for battle – and He will make your arms strong enough to carry heavy loads.
- God will hold you up and provide for your every need.
- God will expand the roads that you travel on – and your feet will not stumble.

Can you imagine this kind of breakthrough? Are you ready for it? Can you see areas in your life where breakthrough is needed? It doesn't just happen, you must cultivate it. David was described as a 'man after God's own heart'. (Acts 13:22) David wasn't perfect, but he was obedient. And every time he fell short, David knew how to bring his brokenness to God. Breakthrough – if you really want it – starts right here, right now...

Keys to Cultivating Breakthrough:

1. **Keep God first**
    Matthew 6:33 - But seek first the kingdom of God and His righteousness, and all these things shall be added to you.

2. **Keep the devil under your feet**
    James 4:7 - Therefore submit to God. Resist the devil and he will flee from you.

3. **Remain broken before God**
    Psalm 51:17 - The sacrifices of God are a broken spirit; A broken and a contrite (repentant) heart, O God, You will not despise.

4. **Watch your words**
    Colossians 4:6 - Let your conversation be always full of grace, seasoned with salt, so that you may know how to answer everyone.

    Ephesians 4:20 - Let no corrupt word proceed out of your mouth, but what is good for necessary edification, that it may impart grace to the hearers.

    Proverbs 31:26 - She opens her mouth with wisdom, And on her tongue is the law of kindness.

    Psalm 141:3 - Set a guard over my mouth, LORD; keep watch over the door of my lips.

5. **Become disciplined in prayer**

    John 15:7 - If you abide in me, and my words abide in you, ask whatever you wish, and it will be done for you.

    Proverbs 14:1 - The wise woman builds her house, But the foolish pulls it down with her hands.

    Philippians 4:16 - Do not be anxious about anything, but in everything by prayer and supplication with thanksgiving let your requests be made known to God.

    Matthew 21:22 - And whatever things you ask in prayer, believing, you will receive."

    1 Thessalonians 5:17 – Pray without ceasing

As we conclude this study, let's take a look at the last verse in Judges 5.

Judges 5:31 (TLB)
"O Lord, may all your enemies
Perish as Sisera did,
But may those who love the Lord
Shine as the sun!"

After that there was peace in the land for forty years.

Did you see that? 'But may those who love the Lord shine as the sun'. Do you know how bright the sun is? According to sciencing.com, the sun provides light, warmth and energy to Earth although it is roughly 93 million miles away. It is said that the sun is so bright because of its *power source*, which is a process called nuclear fusion which yields abundant energy. So, Deborah prayed that those who love the Lord (that includes you) would shine as the sun. And we're able to shine bright because of the power source – God Himself – who lives inside us. (1 Corinthians 3:16, 6:19)

2 Corinthians 4:7 (TLB) ~ *But this precious treasure – this light and power that now shine within us – is held in a perishable container, that is, in our weak bodies. Everyone can see that the glorious power within must be from God and is not our own.*

You were created to shine – it's in your DNA. May you shine as bright as the sun. May your light never become dimmed by life and its circumstances. May your glorious glow provide light in the darkest of days. May your light attract more light – and never cease from shining. May everything that you touch and everything that you do become a reflection of the light that shines in you. May you light up this world for the glory of God.

Matthew 5:14-16 (TLB) ~ You are the world's light—a city on a hill, glowing in the night for all to see. [15-16] Don't hide your light! Let it shine for all; let your good deeds glow for all to see, so that they will praise your heavenly Father.

God called Deborah during unprecedented times to lead the people to an unprecedented victory. It was her *defining moment*. Then, God called an ordinary woman named Jael to carry out an extraordinary responsibility. It was also her *defining moment*. Dictionary.com describes a defining moment as a point at which the essential nature or character of a person is revealed or identified. We are living in a time where a new normal is emerging. Crisis, afflictions, hard-times, and even global pandemics – are all designed to usher us into our defining moment. And the rich significance of a defining moment is not in what you think about it, but in how you respond.

How is God calling you in this season? How will you handle this moment?

Isaiah 60:1 ~

Arise, shine,

For your light has come,

And the glory of the Lord is risen upon you.

This is your moment. The seeds that you've planted, the prayers that you've prayed, the words that you've spoken, the obstacles that you've overcome – it all comes down to this moment. And here's what the Lord is saying: 'Woman, arise! This is only the beginning'.

Dig Deeper

Psalm 84:11 ESV ~ For the Lord God is a sun and shield;
  the Lord bestows favor and honor.
No good thing does he withhold
  from those who walk uprightly.

S — (Scripture)

_____

_____

_____

E — (Examine)

_____

_____

_____

E — (Envision)

_____

_____

_____

D — (Declare)

_____

_____

_____

Thank You
For taking this journey with us!

Connect with us on Facebook and Instagram
@SanctumAndSeed

Contact us:
info@sanctumandseed.com

Visit us at www.SanctumAndSeed.com
to stay in-the-know on all future Bible Study releases and other newsworthy info.

Sanctum
+SEED

www.ingramcontent.com/pod-product-compliance
Lightning Source LLC
Chambersburg PA
CBHW081333090426

42737CB00017B/3115